D0122281

50

great pasta sauces

By Pamela Sheldon Johns

Produced by Jennifer Barry Design

Photographs by Joyce Oudkerk Pool

Andrews McMeel
Publishing, LLC
Kansas City

50 Great Pasta Sauces copyright © 2006 by Pamela Sheldon Johns and Jennifer Barry Design.
Photographs copyright © 2006 by Joyce Oudkerk Pool.

All rights reserved. Printed in Singapore. No part of this book may be used or reproduced
in any manner whatsoever without written permission except in the case of reprints in the
context of reviews. For information, write Andrews McMeel Publishing, LLC,
an Andrews McMeel Universal company, 4520 Main Street, Kansas City, Missouri 64111.

Concept and Design: Jennifer Barry Design, Fairfax, California
Production Assistance: Kristen Wurz
Food Styling: Pouké and Dan Becker

07 08 09 10 TWP 10 9 8 7 6 5 4 3

ISBN-13: 978-0-7407-6178-2
ISBN-10: 0-7407-6178-1

Library of Congress Cataloging-in-Publication data is on file.

www.andrewsmcmeel.com

Attention: Schools and Businesses

Andrews McMeel books are available at quantity discounts with bulk purchase for
educational, business, or sales promotional use. For information, please write to:
Special Sales Department, Andrews McMeel Publishing, LLC, 4520 Main Street,
Kansas City, Missouri 64111

about italian sauces

It is winter as I write this; outside it is cold and trying to snow, and I am dreaming of the bounty of summer: juicy vine-ripened tomatoes, sweet and crunchy bell peppers, delicate zucchini flowers, and voluptuous eggplants . . . I bundle up and go out to wander nostalgically through my Tuscan *orto,* the kitchen garden that was and will again be the provider of the products that supply the foundation to garnish our daily staple, pasta. What I find now in my *orto* is the bounty of winter: garlic, onions, and *cavolo nero*—an almost black kalelike green—still thriving. I grab handfuls of it and run into the kitchen. In a large pan I pour some of my precious homegrown olive oil and start to brown a little pancetta, onion, and garlic. I chop up the *cavolo nero* and add it, with a little broth to moisten it. Soon the house is redolent of sweet and piquant aromas. A pinch of *peperoncino* and a few of the *piennolo* tomatoes that have been hanging since September, slightly dehydrated and still so sweet, and suddenly I am willing to wait for summer.

In Italy, the sauce on pasta is an accessory, the embellishment of available seasonal products to enhance what is the fundamental dish of every Italian meal. It could be as simple as a fresh, fruity olive oil and a shaving of Parmigiano-Reggiano cheese, or as complex as a ragù that has simmered for hours, but the reality is that sauces are treated as a condiment, measured in moderate quantities. Sauce ingredients are determined by several parameters: geography, climate and seasonal ingredients, economy, and history.

The Republic of Italy is a peninsula surrounded by the Mediterranean Sea. The country is divided into twenty regions that have been united for less than 150 years. Each has a unique cuisine indicated by local agriculture and geography. In the past, before transportation was so extensive, these identities remained distinct. Today, with improved conveyance and the advent of the supermarket, interregional products can be found. Tradition and pride in local products are still maintained, however, and dishes have continued to have a strong regional essence.

From top of the boot to toe, the country has wide geographic diversity. Stretching over seven hundred miles from the Alps in the north to the arid, even subtropic, regions of the south, there are hundreds of miles of coastline and the mountainous regions of the Alps and the Apennines. Microclimates abound, and the composition of soil changes dramatically from the humid and fertile plains in the north to the rich volcanic areas in the south.

In general, in the north, the climate is significantly cooler and more humid. The Padano plain stretches across the top of the country, following the Po River, and is considered the heartland of agriculture. Here there are a wealth of industry and numerous dairies and pork producers. Soft wheat is grown here, as well as rice, sugar beets, and soybeans. Sauce preparations make use of the abundance of dairy products, such as cheese, butter, and cream, and cooler-climate vegetables, such as cardoons, radicchio, and sweet peppers.

In the south, the climate is much warmer and drier, and there is a less complex economy. The growing season lasts longer than in the north, and sun-drenched ingredients, such as tomatoes, garlic, broccoli rabe, and eggplant, are found in the typical dishes there. Hard durum wheat and olive oil are staples. In such historically impoverished areas, the tendency has been toward simpler dishes that don't require as much time in a hot kitchen and that utilize the local staples. We think of tomatoes as the classic Italian sauce, but the introduction of tomatoes from the Americas wasn't until the late 1700s.

Pasta has a long history in Italy. From its origins as a simple, inexpensive food that could nourish peasant workers, pasta has evolved to a high art. In most restaurants, the first course, or *primo piatto,* is an indication of the quality of the rest of the meal. It's not just pasta—it's Italy's national dish.

As in the sauces and ingredients, there are important regional differences in pasta. Fresh pasta historically predominated northern regions because the climate is right for growing soft wheat. Soft wheat does not have enough protein to create the gluten needed for a pasta strong enough to stand up to the kneading and drying process, whereas in the south, where high-protein *semola* (semolina), or hard wheat, is grown, the culture of dried pasta has evolved.

Basic dried pasta is, after all, only flour and water. The way those two ingredients are handled can make all the difference in the taste and nutrition of this humble food. Modern industrial methods can produce high volumes of a product that can be found in much of the world, but a few artisanal producers still make it the way it was made in the past. Their secret is in the use of *semola*, good water, the use of bronze extrusion dies (perforated plates for shaping), and slow air-drying at low temperatures.

Bronze dies give the extruded pasta a rough, porous external surface that helps sauce cling to it. Industrial producers, on the other hand, often use Teflon dies. Teflon is easier to clean and squirts out the pasta at a high speed, resulting in a pasta with a hard, slick finish that doesn't interact with sauces.

Air-drying is likewise important to the flavor of the pasta. Industrial producers flash-dry the pasta in high heat over two to four hours, a process that kills flavor and nutrition. Artisanal air-drying is done in warm rooms with constant air circulation, simulating the historic process of sun-drying over a period of days. Luckily, there are now several artisanal dried *paste* imported from Italy (see Sources, page 108).

• • •

Fresh pasta cooks quickly. Angel hair needs only 30 to 45 seconds, fettuccine will take 1 to 2 minutes, and ravioli need 2 to 3 minutes. Dried pasta takes longer, as it needs to rehydrate. Pasta should not be soft or soggy when served. It should have a slight resistance to the bite; the Italians call it al dente, "to the teeth." They believe that pasta cooked al dente is more easily digested and just tastes better.

The best way to test for doneness is to bite into a sample. As you look at a cross-section, you can see that the outer part of a solid piece of pasta (and the inner part of a hollow shape) cooks first; the color changes. The part that is uncooked in the center is still white. When that white is just about to disappear, the pasta is ready. The ambient heat will continue to cook it to just the right consistency by the time it is on the table. If you think you have over-cooked the pasta, immediately add cold water to the pot to stop the cooking.

The recipes in this book are all for moderately sized main-course servings. To determine quantities, allow about 4 ounces of pasta per person.

Cook pasta in a large pot in plenty of water, at least 6 quarts for each pound of pasta being cooked. This keeps the pasta from sticking together. Don't add oil. If the pasta has enough room to move around and is stirred frequently while cooking, it won't stick. Before adding the pasta, liberally salt the water. This really adds to the flavor of the pasta.

I use roughly 2 tablespoons of salt for each pound of pasta. Start with high heat to bring the water to a boil. Add the pasta a little at a time, stirring. As soon as the pasta is added, reduce the heat slightly, maintaining a soft boil. Cook it, uncovered, stirring frequently with a wooden spoon to keep it from sticking. When you think the pasta is done to the right degree, drain it in a colander, reserving a little of the pasta-cooking water for your sauce, if needed.

A few words about the pasta you use: In the following recipes, I have occasionally recommended a specific pasta shape, such as spaghetti for the carbonara sauce. This is the classic pasta for the sauce at its origin. But you can mix and match as you like. Just remember that heavy sauces require a pasta strong enough to hold up to them, and conversely, a light sauce should have a delicate pasta to accompany it.

. . .

The pasta sauces in this book can be considered starting points. You should feel free to substitute whatever is fresh, seasonal, and colorful in the market, or adjust the ingredient amounts to your personal taste. A perfect example is the very basic besciamella (page 46). You may recognize it as béchamel sauce in French, but instead of starting with butter, I use olive oil. The olive oil adds flavor and also doesn't tighten up as the sauce cools; the sauce remains fluid. I consider this my "artist's palette," a clean base to which I can add flavors and colors—pureed spinach, perhaps, or grated Parmigiano-Reggiano, or sometimes a mixture of grilled vegetables or some leftover grilled meat. I also use it to bind together leftover pasta to make a baked pasta dish.

Keep a selection of interesting ingredients in your pantry to provide a quick condiment for your pasta: anchovies, bottarga (dried fish roe), fennel flowers (also called fennel pollen), capers, olives, sun-dried tomatoes, and, of course, excellent extra-virgin olive oil. Each of these unique flavors can give a boost to a pasta sauce. Italian ingredients are more readily available in the United States than they used to be. In the back of the book, I have listed several importers who carefully hand-select products from small artisanal producers.

Allora, buon appetito!

vegetable sauces

broccoli cream sauce

This savory sauce can be put together in short order. Using the broccoli stems gives the sauce substance and flavor.

3 tablespoons extra-virgin olive oil

1 red bell pepper, seeded, deveined, and diced

¼ cup finely chopped onion

2 cloves garlic, minced

2 anchovy fillets

1½ cups chicken stock (page 102)

1 cup peeled and thinly sliced broccoli stems

8 ounces broccoli florets, blanched for 2 minutes (see page 105)

¼ cup mascarpone cheese

1 pound dried pasta

• In a large saucepan, heat the olive oil over medium heat. Add the bell pepper, onion, garlic, and anchovies. Sauté until the vegetables are soft but not brown, 3 to 5 minutes. Remove from the heat and set aside.

• In a medium saucepan, bring the chicken stock to a boil over medium heat. Add the broccoli stems and cook until tender, 6 to 8 minutes. Add half of the blanched broccoli florets and cook for a minute or two to heat through. Puree with a blender and add to the bell pepper mixture. Add the mascarpone, bring to a simmer, and cook, stirring, until the cheese is melted. Add the remaining broccoli florets and cook for a minute or two to heat through. Set aside and keep warm.

• In a large pot of salted boiling water, cook the pasta until al dente. Drain and transfer to a warmed serving bowl. Spoon the broccoli sauce over the top and serve at once. *Serves 6*

basil pesto sauce

Basil pesto is usually made with pine nuts, but you can also substitute walnuts or almonds. Classic Ligurian pesto is made with pine nuts and is often served with a short fresh pasta called trofie.

3 cloves garlic

1 bunch basil, stemmed

¼ cup pine nuts, toasted (see page 105)

½ cup extra-virgin olive oil

¼ cup freshly grated Parmigiano-Reggiano cheese

1 pound fresh or dried *trofie* or pasta of your choice

2 potatoes, peeled, sliced ½ inch thick, and blanched for 4 minutes (see page 105)

8 ounces green beans, cut into 3-inch lengths and blanched for 4 minutes (see page 105)

• To make the pesto: With a food processor running, drop in the garlic. Add the basil and pine nuts and process to a grainy texture. With the machine running, gradually add the olive oil to the desired consistency. Fold in the cheese by hand. Set the pesto aside.

• In a large pot of salted boiling water, cook the pasta until al dente. Add the potatoes and green beans for the last minute of cooking to heat them through. Drain, reserving 1 cup of the pasta-cooking liquid.

• Transfer to the serving bowl and toss the pesto with the pasta, adding the pasta-cooking liquid to the desired consistency. Turn into a warmed serving bowl and serve at once.

Serves 6

classic tomato sauce

Italian cooks use canned tomatoes when fresh tomatoes are not in season. Look for the flavorful San Marzano variety, which comes from the rich soil around Mt. Vesuvius.

2 tablespoons extra-virgin olive oil

1 clove garlic, minced

½ cup finely chopped onion

6 ripe plum tomatoes, peeled, seeded (see page 105), and coarsely chopped

2 tablespoons minced fresh basil

2 tablespoons minced fresh flat-leaf parsley

2 cups chicken stock (page 102)

Sea salt and freshly ground black pepper to taste

1 pound dried or fresh pasta

• In a large, heavy saucepan, heat the oil over medium heat and sauté the garlic and onion until soft but not brown, about 3 minutes.

• Add the tomatoes, basil, parsley, and chicken stock. Simmer, stirring occasionally, until the sauce has thickened, 30 to 45 minutes. Puree the sauce in a blender and return to the pan. Season with salt and pepper. Set aside and keep warm.

• In a large pot of salted boiling water, cook the pasta until al dente. Drain and transfer to a warmed serving bowl. Top with the sauce and serve at once. *Serves 4*

roasted tomato sauce

This is a good way to sweeten early tomatoes. Roasting releases juices that create the perfect sauce for your pasta.

6 large ripe tomatoes, cored and cut
   into wedges
¼ cup extra-virgin olive oil
Sea salt and freshly ground black
   pepper to taste
1 pound dried pasta
8 ounces fresh mozzarella, cut into
   ¼-inch dice
¼ cup julienned fresh basil for garnish

• Preheat an oven to 425°F. Toss the tomato wedges with the olive oil. Season with salt and pepper. Place in a single layer in a baking dish. Roast in the oven until the tomato skins have lightly browned, about 15 minutes.

• In a large pot of salted boiling water, cook the pasta until al dente. Drain and turn into a warmed serving bowl. Toss with the roasted tomatoes and mozzarella. Garnish with the basil and serve at once. *Serves 4*

arrabiata sauce

Arrabiata *means "angry." This pasta is spicy, so perhaps it could be called hot-tempered! It is up to you to determine just how much.*

3 tablespoons extra-virgin olive oil

3 large cloves garlic, minced

1 *peperoncino* (small dried red pepper), or 1 teaspoon red pepper flakes

1 (28-ounce) can whole tomatoes, drained and coarsely chopped

2 tablespoons minced fresh flat-leaf parsley

1 tablespoon minced fresh basil

Sea salt and freshly ground black pepper to taste

1 pound dried pasta

• In a medium sauté pan, heat the olive oil over medium-high heat. Sauté the garlic and *peperoncino* until soft but not brown, 2 to 3 minutes. Add the tomatoes, parsley, and basil. Reduce the heat to a simmer and cook, stirring occasionally, for 10 to 15 minutes, until the sauce is slightly thickened. Season with salt and pepper. Set aside and keep warm.

• In a large pot of salted boiling water, cook the pasta until al dente. Drain and transfer to a warmed serving bowl. Top with the sauce and serve at once. *Serves 6*

garlic tomato sauce

This is the classic sauce from southern Tuscany, where I live. It is called aglione, *named for a type of wild garlic similar to green, or immature, garlic. You can substitute mature garlic, but use half the amount. We eat it with a handmade fresh pasta called* pici.

6 large, very ripe tomatoes, peeled, seeded (see page 105), and coarsely chopped

1 small head green garlic (about 6 immature cloves), sliced

3 tablespoons extra-virgin olive oil

1 or 2 *peperoncini* (small dried red peppers), to taste

¼ cup minced fresh flat-leaf parsley

Sea salt and freshly ground black pepper to taste

1 pound fresh or dried pasta

• In a large saucepan, combine the tomatoes, garlic, olive oil, *peperoncini,* and parsley. Bring to a simmer over medium heat and cook, stirring occasionally, for 30 to 35 minutes, or until the garlic is very tender (mature garlic will take 5 to 7 minutes longer). Season with salt and pepper. Set aside and keep warm.

• In a large pot of salted boiling water, cook the pasta until al dente. Drain, turn into a warmed serving bowl, and toss with the sauce. Serve at once. *Serves 6*

roasted beets sauce

Roasting vegetables sweetens them, and the flavor of beets is especially enhanced by this process. When mixed with the pasta, the beets color this dish an appealing fuchsia.

1 bunch (about 8 small or 3 large) beets
with greens
4 tablespoons extra-virgin olive oil
Sea salt and freshly ground black
pepper to taste
1 pound dried pasta
1 onion, finely chopped

• Preheat the oven to 400°F. Lightly oil a medium casserole.

• Remove the beet leaves and discard the tough stems. Rinse and spin the leaves dry; julienne them and set aside. Trim the root and stem from the beets and scrub well. If using large beets, cut into quarters. In a pot of salted boiling water, cook the beets for 15 minutes, or until fork-tender. Drain, reserving the water, and remove the skins. Put the beets in the prepared casserole and drizzle with 2 tablespoons of the olive oil. Season with salt and pepper. Roast in the oven (or on a grill for a smoky flavor) for 20 minutes, or until lightly browned.

• In a large pot of salted boiling water, cook the pasta until al dente.

• Meanwhile, in a medium sauté pan, heat the remaining 2 tablespoons olive oil over medium heat and sauté the onion until golden brown, 3 to 4 minutes. Add 1 cup of the reserved beet-cooking water and bring to a boil. Cook to reduce the volume by half. Add the julienned beet greens and cook just until wilted.

• Drain the pasta and transfer to a warmed serving bowl. Add the roasted beets and greens. Toss and serve at once. *Serves 4*

asparagus & butter sauce

In the spring, pasta with this sauce is delightful with asparagi selvatici, *the wispy wild asparagus. In Emilia-Romagna, it is enjoyed with fresh* garganelli, *a handmade ridged tube pasta.*

½ cup (1 stick) unsalted butter

1 pound asparagus, blanched for 3 to 5 minutes (see page 105) and cut into 3-inch-long pieces

½ teaspoon sea salt

1 teaspoon freshly ground black pepper

1 pound fresh or dried pasta

½ cup freshly grated (2 ounces) Parmigiano-Reggiano cheese

• In a large sauté pan, melt the butter over low heat. Add the asparagus and toss to coat. Season with the salt and pepper and set aside.

• In a large pot of salted boiling water, cook the pasta until al dente. Drain and turn into a warmed serving bowl. Toss with the asparagus and Parmigiano-Reggiano. Serve at once.

Serves 6

grilled vegetable sauce

This is the perfect summer meal to serve with a fresh green salad and a crisp white wine. The vegetables can also be grilled and marinated ahead, making it a quick weeknight dinner.

½ cup extra-virgin olive oil, plus more
    for brushing

2 shallots, minced

¼ cup balsamic vinegar of Modena

2 Japanese eggplants, cut into
    ½-inch-thick lengthwise slices

6 baby zucchini, trimmed

1 red bell pepper, seeded, deveined, and
    cut into eighths

4 shiitake mushrooms, stemmed and
    halved

12 tiny new potatoes, halved and
    cooked until tender

Sea salt and freshly ground black
    pepper to taste

1 pound dried pasta

• Light a medium-hot fire in a charcoal grill or preheat a gas grill to 375°F.

• In a medium saucepan, heat the ½ cup olive oil over medium-high heat. Add the shallots and cook until soft but not brown, about 4 to 6 minutes. Stir in the vinegar and remove from the heat.

• Brush the eggplants, zucchini, pepper, mushrooms, and potatoes with olive oil. Season with salt and pepper. Grill for 3 to 4 minutes on each side, or until lightly browned.

• Put the vegetables in a shallow dish and pour the balsamic mixture over them. Let stand for 30 minutes at room temperature, or overnight in the refrigerator.

• To serve, if using refrigerated vegetables, let them warm to room temperature. In a large pot of salted boiling water, cook the pasta until al dente. Drain and transfer to a warmed serving bowl. Toss with the vegetables and serve immediately. *Serves 6*

fava bean sauce
with spring vegetables

Use your favorite pasta along with the best seasonal vegetables for this sauce. Small fava beans are quite tender unpeeled and add texture.

1 pound penne, or pasta of your choice

5 tablespoons extra-virgin olive oil

2 pounds fava beans, shelled and blanched for 1 minute (see page 105)

1 red spring onion, diced

1 bunch baby carrots, peeled, halved lengthwise, and blanched for 2 minutes (see page 105)

Sea salt and freshly ground black pepper to taste

1/2 cup freshly grated (2 ounces) Parmigiano-Reggiano cheese

6 zucchini flowers, blanched for 30 seconds (see page 105)

• In a large pot of salted boiling water, cook the pasta until al dente. Drain and reserve 1 cup of the pasta-cooking liquid. Toss the pasta with a tablespoon of the olive oil and set aside in a warm place.

• Remove the skin from two-thirds of the largest fava beans by pinching off the end and squeezing the brightly colored bean out. Reserve the unpeeled beans.

• In a large sauté pan, heat the remaining oil over medium-high heat and sauté the onion for 3 to 4 minutes, or until golden brown. Add the reserved pasta-cooking liquid and bring to a boil. Cook over high heat to reduce to 1/2 cup, then reduce the heat to a simmer; add the carrots and the peeled and unpeeled fava beans. Heat for 3 to 4 minutes, or until the vegetables are warmed through. Season with salt and pepper.

• Transfer the pasta to a warmed serving bowl. Add the vegetable mixture and toss. Stir in the Parmigiano-Reggiano, garnish with the zucchini flowers, and serve at once. *Serves 6*

borlotti bean sauce

This is a hearty pasta e fagioli, *which is usually made with fresh* maltagliati, *the odd-shaped pieces left over from cutting out pasta shapes. For a shortcut, used canned beans, reserving the liquid they are packed in to flavor the sauce, and thinning to the desired consistency with chicken stock.*

1 cup dried borlotti (cranberry) beans

3 cloves garlic

3 fresh sage leaves

3 tablespoons extra-virgin olive oil

1 onion, finely chopped

1 carrot, peeled and finely chopped

1 stalk celery, finely chopped

10 cups chicken stock (page 102)

1 tablespoon minced fresh flat-leaf parsley

1 teaspoon minced fresh thyme

1 pound fresh pasta, cut into 1-inch odd-shaped pieces (page 104), or ribbon pasta

Sea salt and freshly ground black pepper to taste

• Soak the beans with the garlic and sage overnight in water to cover by 2 inches.

• The next day, drain the beans, reserving the garlic and sage. In a large, heavy saucepan, heat the oil over medium heat and sauté the onion, carrot, and celery until golden brown, 6 to 8 minutes. Add the chicken stock, drained beans, garlic, and sage. Bring to a boil, then reduce the heat to a simmer. Add the parsley and thyme and cook, uncovered, for 3 to 3½ hours, or until the beans are tender.

• Add the pasta pieces to the beans and cook until al dente. Season with salt and pepper and serve at once. *Serves 6*

tomato & white bean sauce

This recipe makes a complete meal in one dish.
If you are short on time, you can substitute two
15-ounce cans of cannellini beans for the dried beans.
Be sure to add an extra cup of chicken stock for flavor.

1 cup dried cannellini beans

1 tablespoon minced fresh rosemary,
plus 1 sprig rosemary

3 tablespoons extra-virgin olive oil

1 onion, finely chopped

1 carrot, peeled and finely chopped

1 stalk celery, finely chopped

5 cups rich chicken stock (page 102)

6 tomatoes, cut into quarters lengthwise

Sea salt to taste

8 ounces dried pasta

½ cup (2 ounces) Parmigiano-Reggiano
cheese shavings

• Rinse and soak the beans overnight with the minced rosemary in water to cover by 2 inches.

• Preheat the oven to 250°F. In a large saucepan over medium heat, heat the 3 tablespoons oil

and sauté the onion, carrot, and celery until golden brown, 6 to 8 minutes. Drain the beans and add to the pan along with the chicken stock. Bring to a boil over high heat, then reduce the heat to a simmer. Add the rosemary sprig and cook, uncovered, for about 2 hours, or until the beans are tender but not falling apart.

• Meanwhile, place the tomatoes, cut side up, on a wire rack on a baking sheet. Sprinkle with sea salt and dry in the oven for about 2 hours. They will de-hydrate and intensify in flavor but still be a little soft. Remove the tomatoes from the oven and set aside.

• When the beans and tomatoes are done, cook the pasta in a large pot of salted boiling water until al dente. Drain well and place in a warmed serving bowl. Add the beans, their cooking liquid, and the tomatoes and toss. Sprinkle the Parmigiano-Reggiano shavings over the top. Serve at once. *Serves 6*

orange-caper sauce

This sauce is good with any short tube or shaped pasta. It may also be made using lemon instead of orange. Delicious as a main course, it can also be served as a side dish with grilled seafood or chicken.

¼ cup extra-virgin olive oil

2 large onions, thinly sliced

2 teaspoons grated orange zest

2 cloves garlic, minced

Juice of 1 orange

1 cup chicken stock (page 102)

1 pound short tube or shaped pasta

2 tablespoons capers, drained

¼ cup minced fresh flat-leaf parsley

Sea salt and freshly ground black
pepper to taste

• In a large sauté pan, heat the olive oil over medium heat and sauté the onions until golden, 6 to 8 minutes. Add the orange zest and garlic and cook until softened, 2 to 3 minutes. Add the orange juice and stir to scrape the bottom of the pan. Reduce the heat to low and add the chicken stock. Simmer, uncovered, for 10 minutes, or until slightly reduced.

• Meanwhile, in a large pot of salted boiling water, cook the pasta until al dente, then drain. Toss with the onion mixture; add the capers, parsley, salt, and pepper. Turn into a warmed serving dish and serve at once. *Serves 4*

arugula & pancetta sauce

In the fall, this dish is can be made with cavolo nero, *or Tuscan kale.*

¼ **cup extra-virgin olive oil, plus**

    1 tablespoon for tossing pasta

4 ounces pancetta, diced

1 onion, diced

1 pound fresh or dried pasta

3 cups arugula

Sea salt and freshly ground black

    pepper to taste

• In a medium sauté pan, heat the ¼ cup olive oil over medium-high heat. Sauté the pancetta and onion until golden brown, 5 to 6 minutes. Set aside and keep warm.

• Meanwhile, in a large pot of salted boiling water, cook the pasta until al dente. Drain and toss with the olive oil.

• Add the arugula to the pancetta and cook over medium heat, stirring, just to wilt slightly. Season with salt and pepper. Turn the pasta into a warmed serving bowl, toss with the arugula mixture, and serve at once. *Serves 4*

greens & anchovy sauce

In Puglia, orecchiette are served with a pungent sauce of peppery turnip greens and anchovies.

10 ounces (about 4 cups) turnip greens, julienned

3 tablespoons extra-virgin olive oil

2 cloves garlic, minced

3 anchovy fillets

2 ripe tomatoes, peeled (see page 105) and coarsely chopped

1 *peperoncino* (small dried red pepper)

Sea salt and freshly ground black pepper to taste

1 pound fresh or dried orecchiette, or your choice of dried pasta

• In a large pot of salted boiling water, blanch the turnip greens for 3 minutes (see page 105). Drain and reserve the cooking water to cook the orecchiette.

• In a medium sauté pan, heat the olive oil over medium-high heat. Add the garlic, anchovies, tomato, and *peperoncino*. Sauté for 10 minutes, or until softened, then add the turnip greens and cook for 5 minutes longer, or until the tomatoes are very soft. Remove and discard the *peperoncino* and season the sauce with salt and pepper. Set aside and keep warm.

• Bring the cooking water back to a boil and salt. Add the orecchiette and cook until al dente. Drain and transfer to a warmed serving bowl. Add the sauce and serve at once. *Serves 4*

wild mushroom sauce

This savory autumn sauce can be made with a mixture of any fresh mushrooms available.

2 tablespoons extra-virgin olive oil

2 large shallots, minced

3 cloves garlic, minced

8 ounces mixed wild mushrooms (porcini, shiitakes, and/or chanterelles), stemmed and sliced

2 ounces dried porcini, soaked for 20 minutes in warm water

¼ cup dry Marsala wine

2 cups chicken stock (page 102)

1 pound boneless, skinless chicken breast, cut into julienne strips

1 teaspoon minced fresh thyme

1 tablespoon minced fresh flat-leaf parsley

Sea salt and freshly ground black pepper to taste

1 pound dried pasta

• In a medium sauté pan, heat the olive oil over medium-high heat. Sauté the shallots and garlic until soft but not brown, 2 to 3 minutes. Add the sliced mushrooms. Strain the dried porcini mushrooms and reserve the soaking liquid. Chop the strained mushrooms and add to the sauce. Cook for 10 minutes over medium-high heat, until the mushrooms have softened and the liquid has evaporated.

• Add the Marsala and stir to scrape the bottom of the pan. Cook to reduce the liquid until slightly thickened. Add the chicken stock and reserved mushroom-soaking liquid and bring to a boil. Add the chicken and herbs. Reduce the heat to a simmer, cover, and cook for 18 to 20 minutes, or until the chicken is opaque through-out and the sauce has thickened slightly. Season with salt and pepper. Set aside and keep warm.

• In a large pot of salted boiling water, cook the pasta until al dente. Drain and turn into a warmed serving bowl, spoon the sauce over the top, and serve at once. *Serves 6*

dairy sauces

carbonara sauce

This is a classic sauce, typically served with spaghetti. It is a rich preparation named for the coal miners that it sustained.

2 tablespoons extra-virgin olive oil

1 onion, diced

4 ounces pancetta, diced

4 egg yolks

½ cup heavy cream

1 cup (4 ounces) freshly grated Parmigiano-Reggiano cheese

Sea salt and freshly ground black pepper to taste

1 pound spaghetti

3 tablespoons minced fresh flat-leaf parsley

• In a small sauté pan, heat the olive oil over medium heat and sauté the onion until soft but not brown, about 3 minutes. Add the pancetta and cook until lightly browned. Remove from the heat and set aside to cool slightly.

• In a large bowl, beat the egg yolks, heavy cream, and Parmigiano-Reggiano together. Stir in the cooled onion mixture and season with salt and pepper. Set aside.

• In a large pot of salted boiling water, cook the spaghetti until al dente. Drain the spaghetti and turn into a warmed serving bowl. Toss with the sauce until well coated, sprinkle with parsley, and serve immediately. *Serves 6*

cream sauce

Prosciutto di Parma, the salty, sweet cured meat from Emilia-Romagna, is paired with peas and cream to create a northern Italian classic. Farfalle, or butterfly pasta, is the classic choice for this sauce.

4 tablespoons unsalted butter

1 small spring onion, sliced

1 cup heavy cream

2 cups green peas

Sea salt and freshly ground white
pepper to taste

1 pound farfalle or pasta of your choice

4 ounces thinly sliced prosciutto di
Parma, cut into thin strips

Freshly grated Parmigiano-Reggiano
cheese for serving

• In a medium sauté pan, melt the butter over medium heat. Add the onion and sauté until soft but not brown, about 3 minutes. Add the cream and heat. Stir in the peas and simmer for 3 to 5 minutes, or until the peas are tender. Season with salt and pepper. Set aside and keep warm.

• In a large pot of salted boiling water, cook the pasta until al dente. Drain and transfer to a warmed serving bowl. Add the sauce, toss to coat, garnish with the prosciutto, and serve with Parmigiano-Reggiano on the side. *Serves 4*

browned butter & sage sauce

This quick and delicious northern Italian sauce is easy to make and complements fresh filled or ribbon pasta.

20 fresh sage leaves

½ cup (1 stick) unsalted butter

2 tablespoons extra-virgin olive oil

1 pound fresh filled pasta (ravioli, tortellini, or agnolotti) or ribbon pasta

¼ cup freshly grated Parmigiano-Reggiano cheese

• Set aside 8 sage leaves for garnish and julienne the remaining leaves. In a medium saucepan, melt the butter over medium heat until it foams. Add the olive oil and julienned sage leaves. Cook, stirring, over medium heat until the butter is golden brown—do not burn it! Set aside and keep warm.

• In a large pot of salted boiling water, cook the pasta until al dente. Drain and place in a warmed serving bowl. Pour the butter mixture over the pasta, add the Parmigiano-Reggiano, and toss gently. Garnish with the whole sage leaves and serve at once. *Serves 4*

red pepper besciamella sauce

Besciamella, or white sauce, can be the base of many other sauces. In this version I have added pureed pepper, but you can try a variety of ingredients instead, such as soaked dried porcini, pesto, or grated cheeses. It can also be used to bind together leftover pasta and sauce to make a baked pasta dish.

3 tablespoons extra-virgin olive oil

3 tablespoons unbleached all-purpose flour

1½ cups whole milk, scalded with ½ onion and 1 bay leaf

1 red bell pepper, roasted, skinned (see page 105), and pureed

Sea salt, freshly ground pepper, and freshly grated nutmeg to taste

1 pound dried pasta

2 tablespoons minced fresh flat-leaf parsley

• In a medium saucepan heat the olive oil over medium-high heat. Add the flour and cook, stirring constantly, for 3 to 4 minutes. Do not brown. Remove the onion and bay leaf from the milk and whisk milk into the flour mixture. Bring to a low boil and continue to cook, stirring constantly, to the desired thickness. Stir in the pureed bell pepper, salt, black pepper, and nutmeg. Set aside and keep warm.

• In a large pot of salted boiling water, cook the pasta until al dente. Drain the pasta and transfer to a warmed mixing bowl. Add the sauce and toss to coat well. Turn into a warmed serving bowl, sprinkle with the parsley, and serve immediately. *Serves 4*

white truffle butter sauce

*Since most of us don't have white truffles
handy, this recipe calls for truffle paste. You
may choose to use truffle oil, but be aware that
most truffle oils are synthetically produced. If
you do have a white truffle (lucky you!), use it
as a condiment, shaving it over the hot pasta
just as it is served.*

6 tablespoons unsalted butter

½ teaspoon white truffle paste

**1 pound fresh pasta (page 104), cut
into tagliolini**

**⅓ cup grated (1½ ounces) Parmigiano-
Reggiano cheese**

**Sea salt and freshly ground black
pepper to taste**

Tartufo bianco d'Alba **(fresh white
truffle from Alba), optional**

• In a small saucepan, melt the butter over
medium heat until it foams. Stir in the truffle
paste.

• In a large pot of salted boiling water, cook the
fresh pasta until al dente. Drain, turn into a
warmed serving bowl, and toss with the melted
butter. Sprinkle with the Parmigiano-Reggiano.
Season with salt and pepper. With a truffle
slicer or mandoline, shave thin slices of the
white truffle, if using, over the pasta to cover.
Serve at once. *Serves 4*

walnut pesto sauce

Usually when we think of pesto, it is the traditional Ligurian blend of basil, nuts, Parmigiano-Reggiano, and olive oil. However, Ligurians have another traditional pesto, tocco du noxe, *which is dialect for a "touch of walnuts," an apt name for this creamy pesto.*

2 cloves garlic

4 ounces walnuts, toasted

(see page 105)

⅓ cup extra-virgin olive oil

1 slice country bread, soaked in

⅓ cup milk

¼ cup freshly grated Parmigiano-

Reggiano cheese

Sea salt and freshly ground white

pepper to taste

1 pound fresh or dried pasta

Flat-leaf parsley leaves for garnish

• In a food processor with the motor running, drop in the garlic to mince. Add the walnuts (reserve 2 tablespoons for garnish), olive oil, and bread-milk mixture. Process until smooth. Fold in the Parmigiano-Reggiano by hand. Season with salt and pepper.

• In a large pot of salted boiling water, cook the pasta until al dente. Drain, reserving 1 cup of the pasta-cooking liquid. In a mixing bowl, toss the walnut pesto with the pasta, adding the pasta-cooking liquid to the desired consistency. Turn into a warmed serving bowl, sprinkle with reserved walnuts and parsley, and serve at once. *Serves 4*

balsamic cream sauce

While you wouldn't use costly traditional balsamic vinegar in this recipe, you should try to find a good-quality balsamic vinegar; check the list of ingredients on the bottle for one that contains some cooked grape must and has spent a few years in wood casks. The traditional balsamic can be drizzled on sparingly at the finish.

2 cups heavy cream

1 cup rich chicken stock (page 102)

¼ cup balsamic vinegar of Modena

1 pound fresh potato gnocchi

Traditional balsamic vinegar for

drizzling (optional)

• In a medium saucepan, combine the cream, chicken stock, and balsamic vinegar of Modena. Bring to a simmer over medium heat. Meanwhile, in a large pot of salted boiling water, cook the gnocchi until tender but still slightly firm, or until they rise to the top of the water. Drain, toss with the cream sauce, and transfer to a warmed serving bowl. Drizzle with the traditional balsamic, if using, and serve immediately.

Serves 4

parmigiano-butter sauce

These rich and simple sauces can be put together quickly at the end of a busy day.

1 pound dried or fresh pasta

½ cup (1 stick) unsalted butter, melted, or ½ cup extra-virgin olive oil

½ cup (2 ounces) freshly grated Parmigiano-Reggiano cheese

3 tablespoons minced fresh flat-leaf parsley leaves

• In a large pot of salted boiling water, cook the pasta until al dente. Drain the pasta, transfer to a warmed serving dish, and toss with the melted butter or oil and the Parmigiano-Reggiano. Garnish with the parsley and serve at once. *Serves 6*

creamy goat cheese sauce

½ cup dry white wine

3 garlic cloves, minced

½ teaspoon sea salt

2 cups heavy cream

5 ounces aged creamy goat cheese

1 pound fresh or dried pasta

• In a medium saucepan, combine the wine, garlic, and salt and bring to a boil over medium-high heat. Cook until reduced by half, about 5 minutes. Stir in the cream and goat cheese with a whisk until the cheese has melted. Pass the sauce through a sieve into a bowl and keep warm over hot water.

• Meanwhile, in a large pot of salted boiling water, cook the pasta until al dente. Turn into a warmed serving bowl, toss with the sauce, and serve at once. *Serves 4*

four-cheese sauce

Any combination of soft Italian cheeses will work well in this sauce. Other cheeses might include fresh mozzarella, mascarpone, or provolone.

½ cup heavy cream

¼ cup shredded fontina cheese

2 ounces Gorgonzola cheese, crumbled

½ cup whole-milk ricotta cheese

½ teaspoon minced fresh thyme

Sea salt and freshly ground black pepper to taste

1 pound dried pasta

¼ cup freshly grated Parmigiano-Reggiano cheese

• In a medium saucepan, combine the cream, fontina, Gorgonzola, and ricotta. Warm slowly over low heat, stirring constantly, until the cheeses have melted. Stir in the thyme, salt, and pepper. Set aside and keep warm.

• In a large pot of salted boiling water, cook the pasta until al dente. Drain and transfer to a warmed serving bowl. Spoon the cheese sauce over the top, sprinkle with the Parmigiano-Reggiano, and serve at once. *Serves 4*

ricotta sauce
with grilled vegetables

This is a summer sauce, full of the color of seasonal vegetables. The light and creamy ricotta is the perfect addition to the smoky flavor of the grilled vegetables.

1 eggplant, cut lengthwise into
    ¼-inch-thick slices

Sea salt for sprinkling, plus more
    to taste

Extra-virgin olive oil for brushing

1 red bell pepper, halved, deveined, and
    seeded

1 yellow bell pepper, halved, deveined,
    and seeded

1 red onion, quartered

2 zucchini, cut lengthwise into
    ¼-inch-thick slices

8 ounces dried pasta

1½ cups (12 ounces) whole-milk ricotta
    cheese, lightly beaten

5 to 6 small fresh basil leaves, julienned

Freshly ground black pepper to taste

• Light a fire in a charcoal grill or preheat a gas grill. You can also use a broiler.

• Sprinkle the eggplant slices with salt on both sides and let drain for 30 minutes on a wire rack. Pat dry with paper towels. Brush lightly with olive oil.

• Preheat the broiler, if using. Grill or broil the eggplant and other vegetables on both sides until lightly browned. Transfer to a baking pan and place in the oven to keep warm.

• In a large pot of salted boiling water, cook the pasta until al dente. Drain and toss with the ricotta cheese and basil. Season with salt and pepper. Divide the pasta among 4 warmed serving bowls. Garnish each bowl with assorted grilled vegetables and serve at once. *Serves 4*

fontina sauce

Fontina cheese comes from the northern region of Piemonte, near the Alps. It is usually served with tajarin, *Piemontese dialect for tagliolini. In the fall, it is often found garnished with paper-thin slices of fresh white truffle.*

3 cups (12 ounces) shredded fontina cheese

1 cup milk, heated

4 tablespoons unsalted butter

3 egg yolks, lightly beaten

Sea salt and freshly ground white pepper to taste

12 ounces fresh pasta, cut into tagliolini (page 104)

• In a medium bowl, combine the cheese and milk. Let stand for 30 minutes.

• In a medium, heavy saucepan, melt the butter over low heat (or use a double boiler over simmering water). Add the cheese mixture and whisk until the cheese has melted. Transfer the mixture to a blender. With the machine running, gradually add the egg yolks. Season with salt and pepper and return to the saucepan. Keep warm over very low heat, stirring occasionally.

• In a large pot of salted boiling water, cook the pasta until al dente. Drain, turn into a warmed serving bowl, and toss with the sauce. Serve at once. *Serves 4*

robiola sauce

This is a basic sauce to which your favorite soft cheese can be added: Gorgonzola, mascarpone, goat cheese, or a combination of them. If you have access to Robiola di Roccaverano, a soft creamy cheese from Piemonte, you will find that it makes a silky rich sauce for fresh or dried pasta.

2 cloves garlic, minced

1 shallot, minced

1 cup dry white wine

2 cups heavy cream

4 ounces Robiola di Roccaverano cheese or other soft cheese

1 tablespoon minced fresh thyme

Sea salt and freshly ground white pepper to taste

1 pound dried or fresh pasta

• In a medium, heavy saucepan, combine the garlic, shallot, and wine. Cook over medium heat until reduced to a thick glaze. Add the cream and cook to reduce slightly, about 3 to 4 minutes. Reduce the heat to a simmer and add the cheese, stirring until melted. Add the thyme, salt, and pepper. Set aside and keep warm.

• In a large pot of salted boiling water, cook the pasta until al dente. Drain and transfer to a warmed serving bowl. Toss with sauce and serve at once. *Serves 4*

gorgonzola-walnut sauce

The dolcelatte, *or sweet milk, style of Gorgonzola is a creamier, younger version of this cheese. If you use regular Gorgonzola, bear in mind that it is much stronger; blend it with a little ricotta if you want a milder flavor.*

1 cup whole milk

2 tablespoons heavy cream

6 ounces Gorgonzola *dolcelatte*

1/2 cup walnuts, toasted (see page 105) and chopped

1/2 teaspoon minced fresh rosemary

1 pound dried pasta

• In a medium saucepan, heat the milk and cream over medium heat. Add the Gorgonzola and simmer, stirring until melted. Stir in 1/4 cup of the walnuts and the rosemary; mix well.

• In a large pot of salted boiling water, cook the pasta until al dente. Drain and transfer to a warmed serving bowl. Spoon the cheese sauce over the top, sprinkle with the remaining 1/4 cup walnuts, and serve immediately. *Serves 4*

scamorza & greens sauce

The rich greens in the dish make you feel like you are eating mouthfuls of vitamins! The contrast between the tart greens and the smoky cheese is very appealing.

3 tablespoons extra-virgin olive oil

2 ounces pancetta, diced

½ cup chopped onion

1 large clove garlic, minced

1 *peperoncino* (small dried red pepper), optional

1 pound turnip greens, kale, and/or Swiss chard, coarsely chopped

1½ cups chicken stock (page 102)

1 pound dried pasta

3 ounces smoked scamorza cheese, cubed

• In a large sauté pan, heat the olive oil over medium heat. Add the pancetta and onion and sauté until lightly browned, about 4 to 6 minutes. Add the garlic and *peperoncino* and cook until the garlic is just soft but not brown, 1 to 2 minutes. Add the greens and cook, stirring, for 3 to 4 minutes, or until wilted. Add the chicken stock and cook for 10 minutes, stirring occasionally, to slightly reduce the liquid.

• In a large pot of salted boiling water, cook the pasta until al dente. Drain and transfer to a warmed serving bowl. Add the sauce and toss to coat. Sprinkle with the cheese and serve at once. *Serves 6*

pecorino & pepper sauce

This is one of our favorite quick and delicious preparations using Tuscan sheep's milk cheese. If you aren't able to find cheese from Tuscany, you can use pecorino romano or your favorite aged cheese.

1 pound dried pasta

3 tablespoons extra-virgin olive oil

4 ounces aged pecorino toscano cheese

Freshly ground black pepper to taste

• In a large pot of salted boiling water, cook the pasta until al dente. Drain and transfer to a warmed bowl. Toss with the olive oil and place on individual serving plates. Using a vegetable peeler, shave the pecorino generously over the hot pasta, grind the pepper over the top, and serve immediately. *Serves 4*

meat sauces

bolognese sauce

The stoves in Bologna always have this sauce simmering to serve with their heavenly fresh pasta. Ground meats can also be used in place of the chopped meats. Typically, this sauce is served with fresh tagliatelle, but it is also delightful with dried pasta.

¼ cup extra-virgin olive oil

4 ounces pancetta, minced

1 onion, finely chopped

1 stalk celery, finely chopped

1 carrot, peeled and finely chopped

8 ounces veal, finely chopped

4 ounces pork, finely chopped

½ cup dry white wine

1 cup veal or beef stock (page 103)

1 (12-ounce) can peeled whole
   tomatoes, coarsely chopped

¼ cup heavy cream

Sea salt, freshly ground black pepper,
   and freshly grated nutmeg to taste

1 pound fresh or dried pasta

• In a large, heavy saucepan, heat the oil over medium-high heat. Add the pancetta and vegetables and sauté for 6 to 8 minutes, or until golden.

• Add the chopped meats and sauté until browned, about 8 to 10 minutes. Add the wine and stir to scrape up the browned bits from the bottom of the pan. Increase the heat to high and cook to reduce the liquid by half. Add the stock and tomatoes. Reduce the heat to a simmer and cook, stirring frequently, for 35 to 40 minutes, or until thickened. Stir in the cream and cook for 2 to 3 minutes to heat. Season with salt, pepper, and nutmeg. Set aside and keep warm.

• In a large pot of salted boiling water, cook the pasta until al dente. Drain and turn into a warmed serving bowl, spoon the sauce over the top, and serve at once. *Serves 6*

baked tomato & meatball sauce

This dish can be prepared a day ahead and refrigerated, baked, and then reheated.

sauce

¹/₂ cup extra-virgin olive oil

1 clove garlic, minced

1 onion, diced

1 carrot, peeled and diced

1 stalk celery, diced

1 pound ripe tomatoes, peeled (see page 105) and coarsely chopped

2 cups veal stock (page 103)

Sea salt and freshly ground black pepper to taste

meatballs

8 ounces ground veal

1 egg

¹/₄ cup freshly grated Parmigiano-Reggiano cheese

2 tablespoons minced fresh flat-leaf parsley

2 slices day-old country-style bread, soaked in 1 cup milk

Sea salt and freshly ground black pepper to taste

Unbleached all-purpose flour for dredging

¹/₂ cup extra-virgin olive oil

1 pound dried tube or short shaped pasta

4 ounces provolone cheese, sliced

• Preheat an oven to 375°F. Lightly oil a 9-by-13-inch casserole.

• To make the sauce: In a large sauté pan, heat the olive oil over medium-high heat. Add the garlic, onion, carrot, and celery and sauté until golden brown, 3 to 4 minutes. Add the tomatoes and stock and stir well. Reduce the heat to low, cover, and cook until slightly thickened, about 1½ hours. Season with salt and pepper. Remove from the heat and set aside.

• To make the meatballs: In a medium bowl, combine the ground meat, egg, Parmigiano-Reggiano, parsley, and bread-milk mixture. Blend with your hands until well mixed. Season with salt and pepper. Shape into balls ¾ inch in diameter. Roll lightly in flour to coat evenly.

• In a medium sauté pan, heat the olive oil over medium-high heat. Add the meatballs and cook, turning frequently, until browned on all sides, 8 to 10 minutes. Using a slotted spoon, transfer to paper towels to drain.

• In a large pot of salted boiling water, cook the pasta until al dente. Drain and place in a bowl. Add the sauce and the meatballs and stir to mix. Transfer to the prepared casserole dish. Top with the provolone slices and bake for 30 minutes, or until the cheese has lightly browned. *Serves 6*

rosemary-lamb sauce

Pasta dressed with this sauce makes an excellent hearty main course or a sumptuous offering for a spring brunch buffet.

5 baby artichokes

1 lemon, halved

1 pound boneless lamb sirloin

Sea salt and freshly ground black

    pepper to taste

¼ cup extra-virgin olive oil

1 small onion, thinly sliced

1 cup dry red wine

2 cups veal stock (page 103)

1 (12-ounce) can peeled whole tomatoes

1 tablespoon minced fresh flat-leaf

    parsley

3 sprigs rosemary

½ cup black Italian olives, pitted

1 pound dried pasta

• Trim the tops of the artichokes. Remove the coarse outer leaves. Cut the artichokes into quarters lengthwise. Rub all the cut surfaces with the lemon. Squeeze the lemon halves into a bowl of water and add the artichokes.

• Cut the lamb into 1-inch cubes and season with salt and pepper. In a medium sauté pan, heat the olive oil over medium-high heat and sauté the lamb and onion for 8 to 10 minutes, or until the lamb is browned. Add the wine and stir to scrape up the browned bits from the bottom of the pan. Increase the heat to high and cook to reduce the liquid by half.

• Add the stock and tomatoes (with their juices) and return to a boil. Reduce the heat to a simmer; add the artichokes, parsley, and rosemary. Cover and cook until the artichokes are tender, 45 to 50 minutes. Stir in the olives and season with salt and pepper to taste. Set aside and keep warm.

• In a large pot of salted boiling water, cook the pasta until al dente. Drain and transfer to a warmed serving dish. Toss with the sauce and serve at once. *Serves 6*

summer beef sauce

This cool dish is perfect for lazy summer lunches. It can be made a day ahead but is best served at room temperature.

2 pounds whole beef tenderloin

**Sea salt and freshly ground black
pepper to taste**

3 tablespoons extra-virgin olive oil

3 ounces pancetta, chopped

2 shallots, minced

¼ cup balsamic vinegar of Modena

1½ cups veal stock (page 103)

1 pound dried tube or shaped pasta

• Season the beef liberally with salt and pepper. In a large sauté pan, heat the olive oil over medium-high heat. Brown the whole tenderloin on all sides, about 8 to 12 minutes. Transfer to a cutting board and let cool.

• Add the pancetta to the pan. Reduce the temperature to medium and sauté for 3 to

5 minutes, or until golden brown. Add the shallots and cook until softened but not browned, about 2 minutes longer. Add the balsamic vinegar and stir to scrape the bottom of the pan. Add the veal stock, increase the heat to high, and cook to reduce the liquid by half. Set aside and keep warm.

• In a large pot of salted boiling water, cook the pasta until al dente. Drain and place in a bowl; toss with the sauce, reserving a couple of tablespoonfuls for later. Set aside and let cool to room temperature, stirring occasionally to keep it from sticking together.

• When ready to serve, transfer the pasta to a warmed serving bowl. Slice the cooled steak very thin (the meat will be rare) and arrange on top. Drizzle with the remaining sauce and serve.

Serves 8

pork & black truffle sauce

This recipe is incredible with a fresh black truffle, but it is also good without it. If you don't have a fresh truffle, the best substitute is a flash frozen one, or a truffle preserved in water and salt and packed in a jar or tin. There are also truffle pastes, oils, and powders.

3 tablespoons extra-virgin olive oil

½ cup diced onion

12 ounces boneless pork loin, cut into ½-inch dice

¼ cup dry red wine

3 cups veal stock (page 103)

1 fresh black truffle, sliced paper-thin

Sea salt and freshly ground black pepper to taste

1 pound dried pasta

• In a medium sauté pan, heat the olive oil over medium heat. Add the onion and cook until soft but not brown, about 3 minutes. Add the pork and sauté for 6 to 8 minutes, or until browned. Add the wine and stir to scrape up the browned bits from the bottom of the pan. Cook until reduced by half, about 2 to 3 minutes. Add the veal stock and simmer for 20 to 30 minutes, or until the pork is very tender. Add the truffle, salt, and pepper. Set aside and keep warm.

• In a large pot of salted boiling water, cook the pasta until al dente. Drain and transfer to a warmed serving bowl. Toss with the sauce and serve at once. *Serves 6*

wild boar sauce

Tuscany in the fall means wild boar. A long-simmered ragù is the perfect cold-weather food. I have listed a resource for boar (see page 108), but you can also substitute pork rump or shoulder.

¼ cup extra-virgin olive oil, plus more
  for tossing pasta

1 onion, finely chopped

1 stalk celery, finely chopped

2 carrots, peeled and finely chopped

2 cloves garlic

1½ pounds boneless wild boar leg
  meat, coarsely chopped

2 cups dry red wine

6 large ripe tomatoes, peeled, seeded
  (see page 105), and diced

1 tablespoon juniper berries

1 sprig rosemary

Sea salt and freshly ground black
  pepper to taste

1½ pounds fresh or dried pappardelle
  pasta

• In a medium sauté pan, heat the olive oil over medium-high heat and sauté the vegetables and garlic until golden brown, 5 to 6 minutes. Add the chopped meat and sauté until browned, 3 to 4 minutes. Add the red wine and cook to reduce until thickened, about 8 to 10 minutes.

• Add the tomatoes, juniper berries, and rosemary. Reduce the heat to a simmer and cook, uncovered, stirring occasionally, for 35 to 40 minutes, or until the meat is tender and the sauce has thickened. Season with salt and pepper. Set aside and keep warm.

• In a large pot of salted boiling water, cook the pasta until al dente. Drain and toss with olive oil. Turn into a warmed serving bowl, spoon the sauce on top, and serve at once. *Serves 8*

sausage & pepper sauce
with olives and basil

This is a quick sauce for when you don't have much time, especially if you have roasted and peeled the peppers in advance.

¼ cup extra-virgin olive oil, plus 3
    tablespoons

¼ cup lightly packed fresh basil leaves

2 red bell peppers, roasted, peeled
    (see page 105), and julienned

2 yellow bell peppers, roasted, peeled
    (see page 105), and julienned

1 pound sweet Italian sausages, cut
    into 1-inch lengths

1 cup oil-cured black Italian olives,
    pitted

1 pound dried pasta

• In a blender, combine the ¼ cup olive oil and the basil. Process to a smooth puree. Transfer to a medium bowl. Add the julienned peppers and set aside.

• In a medium sauté pan, heat the 3 tablespoons olive oil over medium-high heat and brown the sausage pieces for 2 minutes on each side. Add the pepper mixture and the olives and heat through. Set aside and keep warm.

• In a large pot of salted boiling water, cook the pasta until al dente. Drain, turn into a warmed serving bowl, and toss with the sauce. Serve at once. *Serves 6*

rabbit & thyme sauce

In the fall hunting season, wild rabbit is used to make a cacciatore sauce. It is tenderized by being marinated, then simmered slowly. You can substitute domestic rabbit, or even chicken.

1 rabbit (about 3 pounds), cut into 6 serving pieces

½ cup extra-virgin olive oil, plus 3 tablespoons

1½ cups dry white wine

1 tablespoon minced fresh thyme

1 teaspoon juniper berries

3 cloves garlic, minced

Sea salt and freshly ground black pepper to taste

1 small onion, chopped

1 pound tomatoes, peeled (see page 105) and coarsely chopped, or 2 cups canned chopped tomatoes

1 pound dried pasta

4 to 6 thyme sprigs for garnish

• Put the rabbit in a large, shallow bowl. In a small bowl, combine the ½ cup olive oil, ½ cup of the wine, the thyme, juniper berries, garlic, salt, and pepper. Pour over the rabbit and toss to coat well. Cover and refrigerate for at least 8 hours or overnight. Turn the pieces occasionally to ensure contact with the marinade.

• In a large sauté pan, heat the 3 tablespoons olive oil over medium heat. Add the rabbit pieces and cook until golden brown on both sides, 10 to 12 minutes. Add the onion, tomatoes, and remaining 1 cup wine. Reduce the heat and simmer uncovered until the rabbit is tender, 40 to 50 minutes.

• In a large pot of salted boiling water, cook the pasta until al dente. Drain and transfer to a warmed serving bowl. Spoon the rabbit sauce over the top, garnish with the thyme sprigs, and serve immediately. *Serves 6*

Note: If substituting chicken, reduce the cooking time, simmering until tender for 30 to 40 minutes.

roasted chicken sauce

This is a hearty one-dish meal, but it can also be a way to use leftover roasted chicken.

1 whole chicken, about 3 pounds,
    cut into 6 to 8 pieces

Flour for dredging

¼ cup extra-virgin olive oil

1 teaspoon minced fresh rosemary

3 cloves garlic, minced

Sea salt and freshly ground black
    pepper to taste

1 cup dry white wine

1 cup chicken stock (page 102)

½ cup black Mediterranean-style olives

1 pound dried pasta

1 teaspoon fennel pollen (optional)

• Preheat an oven to 400°F. Lightly oil a medium-sized roasting pan.

• Rinse the chicken, pat dry, and dredge lightly in flour. Place the chicken pieces in the prepared pan. Drizzle with the olive oil and sprinkle with the rosemary, garlic, salt, and pepper. Place on the upper rack in the oven and roast until lightly browned, 35 to 40 minutes.

• Remove from the oven and add the white wine, chicken stock, and olives to the pan. Return to the oven and roast, turning occasionally to brown the meat on all sides, until tender, 15 to 20 minutes. Using tongs, transfer the chicken to a plate and keep warm. On the stovetop, cook the roasting juices over high heat until reduced by half, about 4 to 5 minutes.

• Meanwhile, in a large pot of salted boiling water, cook the pasta until al dente. Drain and transfer to a warmed serving bowl. Spoon on enough of the reduced roasting juices to moisten the pasta. Top with the chicken pieces, moisten with the remaining roasting juices and olives, sprinkle with fennel flowers, if using, and serve immediately. *Serves 8*

duck sauce

This sauce can be made ahead and reheated to toss with the pasta just before serving. It is great with either fresh or dried pasta.

3 tablespoons extra-virgin olive oil

2 large onions, diced

2 carrots, peeled and diced

1 stalk celery, diced

1 duck (about 3 pounds), skinned,
   boned, and coarsely ground

¼ cup balsamic vinegar of Modena

4 large tomatoes, peeled, seeded (see
   page 105), and coarsely chopped

1 tablespoon minced fresh flat-leaf
   parsley

1 teaspoon minced fresh rosemary

½ teaspoon minced fresh thyme

Sea salt and freshly ground black
   pepper to taste

1½ pounds fresh pasta, cut into
   pappardelle (page 104)

• In a large sauté pan, heat the olive oil over medium heat and sauté the onions, carrots, and celery for 3 to 4 minutes, or until soft but not brown. Add the ground duck meat and sauté for 8 to 10 minutes, or until brown.

• Add the balsamic vinegar and stir to scrape up the browned bits from the bottom of the pan. Add the tomatoes, parsley, rosemary, and thyme. Reduce the heat to a simmer and cook, uncovered, for 20 to 30 minutes, or until thickened. Season with salt and pepper. Set the ragù aside and keep warm.

• In a large pot of salted boiling water, cook the pasta until al dente. Drain and transfer to a warmed serving bowl. Add the sauce and toss well. Serve immediately. *Serves 6*

chicken liver sauce

This is a simple and rich sauce, perfect for a fall or winter pasta.

3 tablespoons unsalted butter

¼ cup finely chopped onion

8 ounces chicken livers, cleaned and coarsely chopped

¼ cup dry Marsala wine

2 cups chicken stock (page 102), heated

Sea salt and freshly ground black pepper to taste

1 pound fresh pasta, cut into tagliatelle (page 104)

2 tablespoons minced fresh flat-leaf parsley

• In a medium sauté pan, melt the butter over medium heat. Add the onion and chicken livers and sauté for 3 to 4 minutes, or until the onion is soft and the liver is firm. Add the Marsala and stir to scrape up the browned bits from the bottom of the pan. Add the stock and cook for 6 to 8 minutes longer, or until the livers are tender and the sauce has slightly thickened. Season with salt and pepper.

• In a large pot of salted boiling water, cook the pasta until al dente. Drain, turn into a warmed serving bowl, and toss with the sauce. Garnish with parsley and serve at once. *Serves 6*

seafood sauces

snapper & herb sauce

You can substitute your favorite fresh fish in this recipe. The cooking time will vary according to the type of fish you use. More delicate fish will need a shorter time and will tend to fall apart, while denser fish will take longer and remain intact, but either way the result will be delicious.

3 tablespoons extra-virgin olive oil

3 cloves garlic, minced

4 ripe tomatoes, peeled (see page 105) and diced

¼ cup tomato sauce

½ cup dry white wine

3 tablespoons minced fresh flat-leaf parsley

5 or 6 small fresh basil leaves

1 teaspoon minced fresh thyme

Pinch of red pepper flakes

½ cup oil-cured black olives, halved and pitted

1½ pounds red snapper fillets

Sea salt and freshly ground pepper to taste

1 pound dried pasta

• In a large sauté pan, heat the olive oil over medium high heat and sauté the garlic until soft but not brown, about 2 minutes. Add the tomatoes, tomato sauce, wine, parsley, basil, thyme, red pepper flakes, and olives. Reduce the heat to a high simmer and add the fish. Cook for 2 to 3 minutes on each side, or until opaque throughout. Season with salt and pepper. Set aside and keep warm.

• In a large pot of salted boiling water, cook the pasta until al dente. Drain and transfer to a warmed serving bowl. Spoon the snapper and sauce over the top and serve immediately.

Serves 4

lemon-tuna sauce

It doesn't seem possible that cooking the lemon with its skin will taste good, but it does!

**¼ cup extra-virgin olive oil, plus
  3 tablespoons**

1 onion, coarsely chopped

1 lemon, thinly sliced and seeded

Juice of 1 lemon

1 cup vegetable stock (page 103)

12 ounces tuna, cut into 1-inch chunks

1 pound dried pasta

**2 tablespoons brine-packed capers,
  drained**

¼ cup minced fresh flat-leaf parsley

**Sea salt and freshly ground black
  pepper to taste**

• Prepare a fire in a charcoal grill or preheat a gas grill to 375°F, or preheat the broiler.

• In a large sauté pan, heat the ¼ cup olive oil over medium heat and sauté the onion until soft but not brown, 3 to 4 minutes. Add the lemon slices and cook until softened, 2 to 3 minutes. Add the lemon juice and stir to scrape the bottom of the pan. Reduce the heat to a simmer and add the vegetable stock. Reduce the heat to low and cook for 10 minutes, or until slightly reduced.

• In a large sauté pan, heat the 3 tablespoons olive oil over high heat. Add the tuna and cook for 4 to 6 minutes, stirring to sear the outside of the chunks while the inside remains medium-rare. Add to the lemon mixture. Set aside and keep warm.

• Meanwhile, in a large pot of salted boiling water, cook the pasta until al dente. Drain and transfer to a warmed serving bowl. Toss with the tuna mixture; add the capers, parsley, salt, and pepper. Serve at once. *Serves 4*

swordfish & caper sauce

Capers are the flower buds of a scrubby Mediterranean plant that literally grows out of the rocks. The best capers are from the sun-drenched islands off Sicily and are preserved in coarse sea salt to maintain their plumpness and flavor.

8 ounces swordfish, cut into ½-inch-thick slices

Extra-virgin olive oil for brushing, plus 2 tablespoons

Sea salt and freshly ground black pepper to taste

½ cup finely chopped onion

¼ cup salt-cured capers, rinsed and drained

¼ cup coarsely chopped green olives

1 tablespoon red wine vinegar

1 ripe tomato, peeled, seeded (see page 105), and coarsely chopped

1 tablespoon minced fresh flat-leaf parsley

1 pound dried pasta

• Prepare a fire in a charcoal grill, or preheat a gas grill to 375°F. Brush the swordfish with olive oil and season with salt and pepper. Grill for 4 to 6 minutes on each side, or until grill-marked, firm to the touch, and opaque throughout. Transfer to a cutting board, let cool, then cut into chunks.

• In a medium bowl, combine the onion, capers, olives, the 2 tablespoons olive oil, the vinegar, tomato, and parsley. Add the swordfish and toss to mix well. Set aside.

• In a large pot of salted boiling water, cook the pasta until al dente. Transfer to a warmed serving bowl and top with the swordfish mixture; toss well and serve at once. *Serves 4*

anchovy & radicchio sauce

This is the sauce for the classic Venetian bìgoli, a dried pasta made with whole-wheat flour and a bìgolaro, a simple Venetian extrusion device. If you don't have bìgoli, you can substitute whole-wheat spaghetti. The classic radicchio from the Veneto is the long Treviso variety, but the small heads of red radicchio will also work well.

¼ **cup extra-virgin olive oil**

¼ **cup finely chopped onion**

8 ounces anchovy fillets

½ **pound radicchio, shredded**

1 cup dry white wine

Freshly ground black pepper to taste

1 pound *bìgoli* or whole-wheat spaghetti

¼ **cup minced fresh flat-leaf parsley, for garnish**

• In a heavy medium saucepan, heat the oil over medium heat. Add the onion and anchovies (reserving 6 for garnish), cover, and simmer for 10 minutes. Add the radicchio and sauté 4 to 6 minutes, until softened. Add the wine and stir to scrape the bottom of the pan. Continue to simmer 20 minutes longer, or until the anchovies are falling apart and the sauce is creamy. Season with pepper. Set aside and keep warm.

• In a large pot of salted boiling water, cook the pasta until al dente. Drain, turn into a warmed serving bowl, and toss with the sauce. Garnish with the reserved anchovies and the parsley and serve at once. *Serves 6*

pepper & anchovy sauce

In southern Italy, this sauce is often served over large pasta shells filled with spinach and ricotta.

3 tablespoons extra-virgin olive oil

2 cloves garlic, minced

1 onion, finely chopped

2 cups chicken stock (page 102)

6 ripe plum tomatoes, peeled (see
    page 105) and coarsely chopped

3 red bell peppers, roasted, peeled
    (see page 105), and coarsely chopped

3 anchovy fillets

¼ cup minced fresh flat-leaf parsley

Sea salt and freshly ground black
    pepper to taste

1 pound dried pasta

• In a medium sauté pan, heat the olive oil over medium-high heat. Add the garlic and onion and sauté for 2 to 3 minutes, until the onion is soft but not brown. Add the chicken stock, tomatoes, bell peppers, anchovies, and parsley and simmer until sauce has reduced and thickened, 30 to 45 minutes. In a blender, puree the sauce until smooth. Return the sauce to the pan and season with salt and pepper. Set aside and keep warm.

• In a large pot of salted boiling water, cook the pasta until al dente. Drain, turn into a warmed serving bowl, toss with the sauce, and serve at once. *Serves 6*

shellfish sauce

The long coastline of Italy affords a variety of seafood. Create your own combination of shell-fish according to what is fresh at your market. Using spaghetti di nero, *which is seasoned with the black ink from squid, will increase the wonderful seafood flavor of this dish.*

3 tablespoons extra-virgin olive oil

8 jumbo shrimp, shelled and deveined

8 clams, scrubbed

8 mussels, scrubbed and debearded

2 cups dry white wine

2 shallots, minced

1 cup vegetable stock (page 103), heated

1/2 cup heavy cream

Sea salt and freshly ground white pepper to taste

1 pound fresh or dried pasta

• In a large sauté pan, heat the olive oil over medium heat. Add the shrimp, clams, and mussels. Cover and cook for 4 to 5 minutes, or until the clams and mussels have opened. Using a slotted spoon, transfer the shellfish to a bowl. Discard any clams or mussels that have not opened. Add the wine and shallots to the pan and cook to reduce until the liquid is thickened, 6 to 8 minutes. Add the vegetable stock and cream and cook over medium heat until slightly thickened, about 10 minutes. Season with salt and pepper.

• Meanwhile, in a large pot of salted boiling water, cook the pasta until al dente. Drain and transfer to a warmed serving bowl. Add the sauce and toss well. Top with the shellfish and serve immediately. *Serves 4*

clam sauce

In August, Italians flock to the seaside to enjoy the spectacular fresh seafood. One of their favorites is pasta with fresh clams.

2 dozen clams, scrubbed

½ cup dry white wine

½ cup water

1 sprig rosemary, plus 1 teaspoon
  minced fresh rosemary

8 cloves garlic

1 small onion, diced

1 large carrot, peeled and diced

1 stalk celery, diced

2 ripe tomatoes, peeled and seeded
  (see page 105)

1 tablespoon minced fresh thyme

2 tablespoons minced fresh flat-leaf
  parsley

Sea salt and freshly ground black
  pepper to taste

1 pound fresh or dried pasta

• In a large pot, combine the clams, wine, water, and rosemary sprig. Cover and cook over low heat for about 15 minutes, or until the clams pop open. Discard any that don't open. Using a slotted spoon, transfer the clams to a bowl. Strain the broth and return it to the pot.

• Bring the broth to a boil and add the garlic, onion, carrot, celery, and tomatoes. Reduce the heat to medium and cook until the vegetables are tender, about 10 minutes. Add the thyme, parsley, minced rosemary, salt, and pepper. Add the clams and heat for about 3 to 5 minutes, until warmed through.

• In a large pot of salted boiling water, cook the pasta until al dente. Drain and transfer to a warm serving bowl. Ladle the clams and their sauce over the top and serve at once. *Serves 6*

garlic shrimp & wine sauce

This sauce highlights ingredients from the southern Italian coast: sweet shrimp; plump garlic; intense tomatoes from the volcanic soil; and bottarga, a small brick of pungent dried mullet or tuna roe, which is shaved or grated over pasta at the table.

½ cup extra-virgin olive oil

4 cloves garlic, minced

1 *peperoncino* (small dried red pepper), crushed

10 ounces medium shrimp, shelled (reserve shells)

2 zucchini, sliced

2 tablespoons unsalted butter

1 small onion, quartered

1 cup dry white wine

¼ cup minced fresh flat-leaf parsley

1 pound cherry tomatoes, halved

Sea salt and freshly ground black pepper to taste

1 pound dried pasta

Bottarga, to taste

• In a medium bowl, combine the olive oil, garlic, and *peperoncino*. Add the shrimp and zucchini and toss to coat well. Set aside.

• In a medium sauté pan, melt the butter over medium-high heat. Add the onion and shrimp shells and cook until the onion is golden brown, 3 to 5 minutes. Add the wine and cook to reduce until thickened. Remove the shrimp shells and discard, leaving as much of the onion in the pan as possible. Add the shrimp mixture and sauté for 3 to 5 minutes, or until the shrimp are pink and the zucchini has softened. Stir in the parsley and tomatoes. Season with salt and pepper. Set aside and keep warm.

• In a large pot of salted boiling water, cook the pasta until al dente. Drain and transfer to a warmed serving bowl. Toss with the sauce. Grate bottarga over the top and serve at once.

Serves 6

basics

chicken stock

One 3-pound chicken, cut up, or 3 pounds
  chicken parts
1 carrot, peeled and cut into ½-inch pieces
1 stalk celery, cut into ½-inch pieces
1 onion, cut into ½-inch pieces
Bouquet garni: 1 sprig parsley, 1 bay leaf,
  1 sprig thyme, and 4 to 5 peppercorns,
  tied in a cheesecloth square
1 gallon spring water

• In a large stockpot, combine all the ingredients and bring to a boil. Reduce the heat to a simmer and cook, uncovered, for 2 hours, periodically skimming off the foam. Strain, discarding the chicken and vegetables. Let cool, then cover and refrigerate overnight. Remove the congealed fat. Refrigerate for up to 3 days, or freeze for up to 3 months. *Makes 5 quarts*

Rich Chicken Stock: Continue to cook to reduce to half the volume, 2½ quarts.

vegetable stock

¼ cup extra-virgin olive oil

2 onions, coarsely chopped

2 carrots, peeled and coarsely chopped

3 stalks celery, coarsely chopped

½ cup dry white wine

1 gallon spring water

Bouquet garni: 1 sprig parsley, 1 sprig thyme, 1 bay leaf, and 4 or 5 black peppercorns, tied in a cheesecloth square

• In a large stockpot, heat the olive oil over medium heat and sauté the onions, carrots, and celery for 5 to 8 minutes, or until browned. Add the wine, increase the heat to high, and stir to scrape the bottom of the pan.

• Continue cooking until the wine is almost completely evaporated, about 10 to 12 minutes. Add the water and bouquet garni. Bring to a boil, reduce the heat to a simmer, and cook for at least 45 minutes, or until well flavored. Strain the stock and discard the vegetables. Let cool and refrigerate. Store in the refrigerator for up to 3 days, or freeze for up to 3 months. *Makes 3 quarts*

veal or beef stock

6 pounds beef or veal shank bones, cut into 3-inch lengths

2 onions, cut into 1-inch pieces

2 carrots, peeled and cut into 1-inch pieces

1 stalk celery, cut into 1-inch pieces

Bouquet garni: 1 sprig parsley, 1 sprig thyme, 1 bay leaf, and 4 or 5 black peppercorns, tied in a cheesecloth square

10 quarts water

• Preheat the oven to 425°F. Put the bones and onions in a lightly oiled roasting pan and roast, turning occasionally, until very brown, 35 to 40 minutes.

• In a large stockpot, combine the bones, onions, and all the remaining ingredients and bring to a boil. Reduce the heat to medium and simmer, uncovered, for 3 hours, skimming occasionally.

• Strain the stock into another container and discard the solids. Let cool, cover, and refrigerate overnight. Remove the congealed fat. Store in the refrigerator for up to 3 days or freeze for up to 3 months. *Makes 5 quarts*

pasta dough

3 cups unbleached all-purpose flour

4 eggs

1 tablespoon extra-virgin olive oil

• Put the flour in a food processor. In a small container with a pour spout, whisk the eggs with the oil.

• With the machine running, gradually add the egg mixture to the flour until the dough starts to come away from the sides of the workbowl. Process for 30 seconds and check the consistency. The dough should be moist enough to pinch together, but not sticky. Continue to add the egg mixture to the desired consistency, if necessary.

• On a lightly floured surface, knead the dough to form a ball. Place in a self-sealing plastic bag to rest for at least 15 minutes.

• Divide the dough into 4 pieces and roll out one piece at a time, keeping the remaining dough in the plastic bag to avoid drying it out. Using a hand-cranked pasta machine, start on the widest setting. Put the pasta through 8 to 10 times, folding it in half each time, until the dough is smooth. If the dough tears, it might be too wet; dust it with flour, brushing off the excess. Continue putting the dough through the rollers, without folding it, using a narrower setting each time, until the dough is thin enough that you can see your hand through it. Allow the rolled dough to dry on a lightly floured surface while rolling each remaining piece. Cut the dough into the desired pasta shape. *Makes 1 pound*

Notes: To make the dough by hand, mound the flour on a work surface. Make a well in the center and add the eggs and oil. With a fork, beat the eggs and oil together, then gradually blend the flour into the egg mixture. Clean the work surface and flour it lightly. Knead the dough for 10 to 15 minutes, or until smooth and elastic.

To cut the pasta into tagliolini, slice strands to about ⅛ inch wide.
To cut the pasta into tagliatelle, slice strands to about ¼ inch wide.
To cut the pasta into pappardelle, slice strands to about ½ inch wide.

preparation tips

To Toast Nuts: Put the nuts on a baking sheet and toast in a preheated 350°F oven for 8 to 10 minutes, or until golden brown and aromatic. Pine nuts take less time, about 5 to 7 minutes.

To Blanch Vegetables: Drop the vegetables in salted boiling water and cook for the time given in the recipe; transfer immediately to ice water to stop the cooking.

Peeling and Seeding Tomatoes: Cut out the core of each tomato. Drop the tomatoes in a pot of boiling water and blanch for 30 seconds; transfer immediately to ice water to stop the cooking and release the peels, which will slip off in your hands. To seed, cut the tomatoes in half and squeeze out the seeds.

Roasting and Skinning Bell Peppers: Place whole peppers directly over a high flame. If you do not have a gas stovetop, use a grill or put the peppers on a baking sheet under your broiler. Turn the peppers frequently until blackened all over. Place them in a brown paper bag to steam and cool down. Peel the peppers by scraping the blackened skin off with a sharp knife. Remove the stem and seeds before cutting as directed in the recipe.

equivalents

weights and measures

	liquid	dry	liquid	dry
1 teaspoon	⅓ tablespoon			5 grams
1 tablespoon	3 teaspoons			15 grams
2 tablespoons	⅛ cup	1 ounce	¼ deciliter (dL)	30 grams
4 tablespoons	¼ cup	2 ounces	½ dL	60 grams
5⅓ tablespoons	⅓ cup			75 grams
16 tablespoons	1 cup			200 grams
2 cups	1 pint	1 pound	½ liter	450 grams
2 pints (pt)	1 quart (4 cups)	32 ounces	1 liter	900 grams

dry ingredients

Ounces	Grams	Grams	Ounces
1	28.35	1	0.035
2	56.70	2	0.07
3	85.05	3	0.11
4	113.40	4	0.14
5	141.75	5	0.18
6	170.10	6	0.21
7	198.45	7	0.25
8	226.80	8	0.28
9	255.15	9	0.32
10	283.5	10	0.35

liquid ingredients

Ounces	Milliliters	Milliliters	Ounces
1	29.573	1	0.034
2	59.15	2	0.07
3	88.72	3	0.10
4	118.30	4	0.14
5	147.87	5	0.17
6	177.44	6	0.20
7	207.02	7	0.24
8	236.59	8	0.27
9	266.16	9	0.30
10	295.73	10	0.33

Quarts	Liters	Liters	Quarts
1	0.946	1	1.057
4	3.79	4	4.23

Gallons	Liters	Liters	Gallons
1	3.785	1	0.264

acknowledgments

Once again, I want to thank my book partner, Jennifer Barry, for her intuition and creativity, and our publisher, Kirsty Melville, for her confidence in our projects. Our editor, Jean Lucas, and copyeditor, Carolyn Miller, helped guide the book to publication, while photographer Joyce Oudkerk Pool, photo assistant Jami Witherspoon, and food stylists Pouké and Dan Becker brought the dishes gloriously to life.

Thanks seems an insufficient word for my husband, Courtney, the backbone of our active Tuscan life, who quietly keeps things in balance. And, finally, an acknowledgment to my mother, who, at ninety-two years old, is happily taste-testing our recipes again, and to Andreea Farcasescu, who is a treasure.

sources

A. G. Ferrari
(stores in northern California)
Catalog: 877-878-2783
Web site: www.agferrari.com
Importer of artisanal Italian foods, such as pasta, oils, vinegars, spices, and capers.

D'Artagnan
Tel.: 800-327-8246
Fax: 973-465-1870
Web site: www.dartagnan.com
Game, such as hare, boar, and duck; seasonal specialties, such as mushrooms and truffles.

Fra'Mani Handcrafted Salumi
Tel.: 510-526-7000
Web site: www.framani.com
Chef Paul Bertolli's handmade Italian-style salumi.

Gustiamo
Tel.: 877-907-2525
Fax: 718-860-4311
Web site: www.gustiamo.com
Imported Italian artisanal products, such as capers, bottarga, pasta, anchovies, preserved vegetables, oils, and vinegars.

Manicaretti
5332 College Avenue, No. 200
Oakland, CA 94618
Tel: 800-799-9830
Web site: www.manicaretti.com
Importer of artisanal Italian foods, such as pasta, olives, capers, vinegars, salt, anchovies, bottarga, fennel pollen, oregano, and a special Sicilian sun-dried tomato paste.

Market Hall Foods
Tel: 888-952-4005
Fax: 510-652-4669
Web site:
www.markethallfoods.com
A high-quality selection of Italian pasta, oils, vinegars, cheeses, and spices.

Niman Ranch
Tel: 866-808-0340
Fax: 510-808-0339
Web site: www.nimanranch.com
High-quality fresh and cured domestic meats.

Sur La Table (stores nationwide)
Catalog: 800-243-0852
Web site: www.surlatable.com
Italian foods, such as pasta, oils, vinegars, spices, capers, and cookware.

Williams-Sonoma
(stores nationwide)
Catalog: 800-541-2233,
877-812-6235
Web site:
www.williams-sonoma.com
Italian foods, such as pasta, oils, vinegars, spices, capers, and cookware.

Learn to Cook in Italy:

Italian Food Artisans/Culinary Arts, Intl.
U.S. office: Tel: 805-963-7289
Fax: 805-456-0653
Web site: www.FoodArtisans.com
E-mail: Pamela@FoodArtisans.com
Wine and food workshops with the author in several regions of Italy; bed-and-breakfast at the author's farm in Montepulciano (Tuscany).

index